This edition first published in MMXVII by
Book House

Distributed by Black Rabbit Books
P.O. Box 3263
Mankato
Minnesota MN 56002

Cataloging-in-Publication Data is available
from the Library of Congress

Printed in the United States
At Corporate Graphics,
North Mankato, Minnesota

9 8 7 6 5 4 3 2 1

ISBN: 978-1-911242-04-8

BEE

Kevin Ingram

UP CLOSE & SCARY

BOOK HOUSE

Contents

Bees

A hive can hold 60,000 to 80,000 bees.

Bees are furry, flying insects. There are thousands of different species. Honeybees and bumblebees live in groups called colonies. The worker bees build the hive or nest, where their queen lays her eggs. She will stay there with her larvae. The worker bees feed and care for them. They collect pollen and nectar from flowers. The pollen is fed to the larvae and nectar is made into honey.

Usually only worker bees are seen flying around.

Black and yellow stripes send out a warning to predators—bees sting!

The Body

The thick fuzzy hair on a bee's body helps to keep it warm. The body has three main parts: the head, thorax, and abdomen. A hard outer layer, called an exoskeleton, protects the bee's body.

Superpowers

When a honeybee finds food, it does a "bee-dance." It waggles its body and flies in a pattern. This dance tells the other bees where to find food.

By waggling its body, the bee shows how far away the food is.

If the food is close to the hive, the bee flies in circles.

The angle of the bee's dance in relation to the sun tells other bees the direction of the food.

Bees can also use their waggle dance to tell other bees if there are any dangerous predators near the food source.

The Abdomen

The abdomen contains two stomachs. One stomach is for eating nectar. The other carries nectar back to the hive to make into honey. The bee also has a sharp stinger at the end of its abdomen.

A honeybee only stings once. Its stinger is hard to pull out again. As it flies away, the stinger is ripped from the bee's body. This kills it.

Bees only sting if they sense danger.

The stinger has two rows of saw-toothed hooks or blades to cut through the victim's skin.

The stinger hooks are angled. Once they are in a victim's body, they are hard to pull out.

Superpowers

Bees don't need maps! They can sense the Earth's magnetic field. That is like having a built-in compass to show the bee which way to go.

11

The Antennae

A bee uses its antennae to smell, taste, and feel. The antennae can also sense the direction and speed of the wind. This helps bees to fly faster and to work out where to land.

Superpowers

Scientists think bees use their right antenna to spot bees from their own colony.

Tiny hairs on the antennae detect scents and vibrations.

12

A smell is stronger to the antenna that is closer to it.

Bumblebees and honeybees have a joint in their antennae. This allows them to bend in different directions.

Antenna

13

The Eyes

Bees have five eyes—three simple eyes and two compound eyes. The big compound eyes help the bee to see detail and movement. The simple eyes, called ocelli, help the bee to navigate when flying.

Superpowers

The bee's simple eyes can see ultraviolet (UV) light. Many flower petals have ultraviolet-lined patterns on them. These lines guide the bee toward the flower's nectar stores. 14

Compound eyes are made up of thousands of tiny lenses called ommatidia.

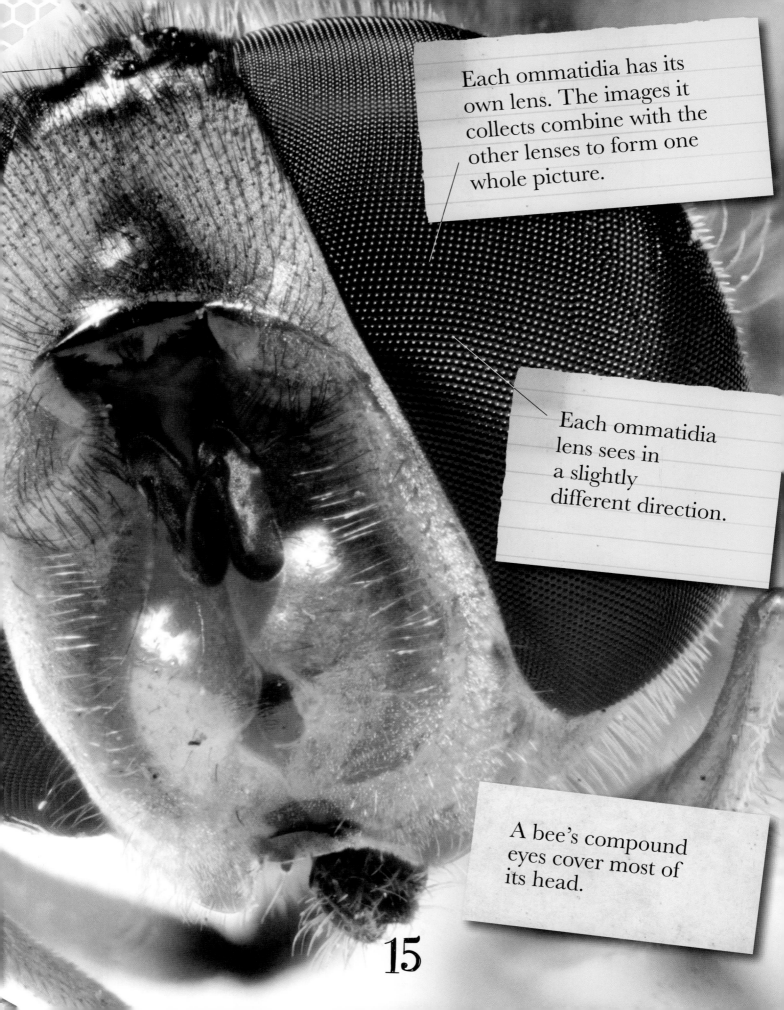

Each ommatidia has its own lens. The images it collects combine with the other lenses to form one whole picture.

Each ommatidia lens sees in a slightly different direction.

A bee's compound eyes cover most of its head.

15

The Mouth

Bees chew wax in their mouth to soften it. They have strong jaws, called mandibles, to cut and shape it. The wax is then turned into the honeycomb of cells inside the hive. The bee has a long, stretchy tongue.

Mandible

A bee uses its mandibles to feed the queen and larvae. They are also used for cleaning, fighting, grooming, and eating.

Labial palp

Maxilla

There are hairs on the tip of the bee's tongue. This helps it lap up nectar, honey, or water.

Tongue

The bee's stretchy tongue curls up when not in use.

Superpowers

A bumblebee's tongue can stretch to 0.8 inches (2 cm) long. That means its tongue is as long as its body.

The Wings

Bees have two pairs of transparent wings and can fly at about 16 mph (25 kph). Bees' wings beat between 200 and 230 times each second. They beat so fast that bees can hover in one spot.

Bee wings are transparent but they can look silvery when light strikes them at an angle.

Superpowers

Bees usually fly about 1 mile (1.6 km) from the hive each day. They can fly up to 5 miles (8 km) to collect food.

If the hive gets too hot, bees flap their wings at the entrance. This wafts in cooler air.

The bee's front wings are bigger than its back wings.

It is the bee's fast beating wings that create the buzzing sound.

19

The Legs

Bees have six legs. Each leg has five joints in it. Bees use their back legs to carry pollen to the hive. They can rub their front legs over their antennae to clean off pollen and dust.

Hairs on the back legs help the bee collect pollen.

This is a press that helps the bee to pack pollen into the pollen baskets.

Worker bees can carry a big pouch of pollen on each back leg.

This small groove is used to remove pollen from the bee's antennae.

Each leg has a claw to grip and hold things.

Superpowers

A bee's "cargo" of nectar and pollen can weigh as much as the bee itself. An airplane could not fly with such a heavy load.

Queen Bee

Most hives have only one queen. The queen bee is much bigger than the worker bees. She mates with bees called drones and lays her eggs in the hive. The queen's only job is to lay eggs.

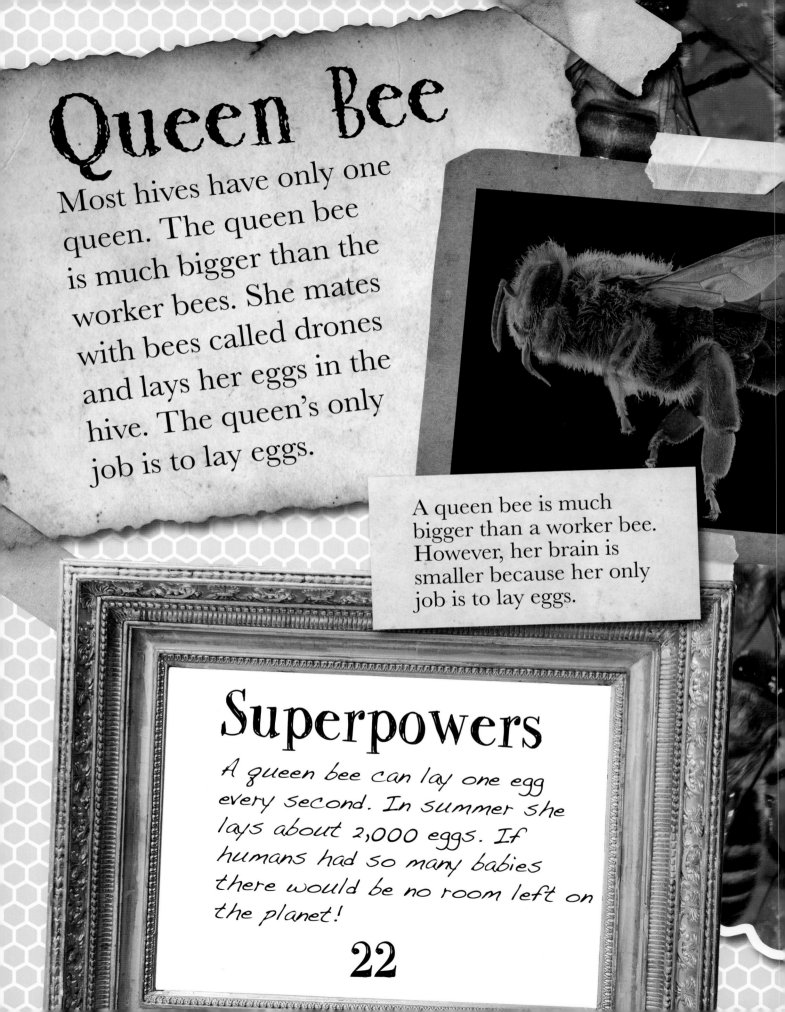

A queen bee is much bigger than a worker bee. However, her brain is smaller because her only job is to lay eggs.

Superpowers

A queen bee can lay one egg every second. In summer she lays about 2,000 eggs. If humans had so many babies there would be no room left on the planet!

22

If the queen dies, a larvae is chosen to replace her. Fed on royal jelly, it will grow into a queen.

Queen bee

The queen bee releases scents called pheromones. This lets her colony know that she is alive and well.

Leafcutter Bees

Leafcutter bees live alone. They build nests in holes in rotting wood or in plant stems. The leafcutter bee bites off pieces of leaves. It uses them to build cell walls inside its barrel-shaped nest.

Leafcutter bees are black and about the size of a honeybee.

A leafcutter bee collects pollen under its abdomen so it looks yellow.

Superpowers

Leafcutter bees are strong enough to fly and carry pieces of leaves. Some pieces are as big, if not bigger, than the bees.

Leafcutters bite very neat circles or ovals from leaves.

Killer Bees

Africanized honeybees are called killer bees because they are so dangerous! A whole colony will attack if its hive is disturbed. That can mean up to 2,000 stings from a large swarm.

Superpowers

When a killer bee stings, it gives off a scent. This sends a signal to the whole colony to swarm and attack. Killer bees will chase people for about 0.25 miles (0.4 km) before stopping.

Once disturbed, a colony can be ready to attack for up to 24 hours.

The "alarm" scent given off by killer bees is called pheromones. It smells like bananas.

It does not take much for killer bees to be disturbed and for their alarm systems to be activated.

Killer bees were created by scientists in Brazil. They mated African and European honeybees to produce bees that made more honey. All they created was very angry bees!

That's Scary!

Bees are dying out—that's scary! In the United States more than half of all honeybee hives have disappeared. Some bees are dying because of climate change. As parts of the world become hotter, heat is killing the bees. Their habitat is also shrinking. Bees have fewer places to nest and fewer flowers to visit.

Superpowers

It takes a long time to make honey. A worker bee lives for around six weeks. About 12 bees can make one teaspoon of honey in that time.

28

Bees are vital to us. They pollinate three quarters of the world's most important crops. We need bees!

Glossary

Abdomen stomach.

Antennae a pair of sense organs located near the front of an insect's head.

Climate change the gradual increase in the Earth's temperature, thought to be caused by human actions, such as burning oil, gas, and coal.

Colonies groups.

Compound eyes eyes made up of many lenses.

Exoskeleton the hard outer covering on the outside of an animal's body.

Groom to clean or brush dust and dirt from an animal's body.

Hives nests built by bees.

Honeycomb a structure of hexagonal cells of wax that forms the inside of a hive.

Insects animals with six legs and a body that is divided into three sections: head, thorax, and abdomen. Some insects also have wings.

Joint a place where two bones or body parts that can move separately, meet.

Larvae the wingless, often worm-like, form of insects when first hatched from eggs.

Lens the part of an eye that gathers light so an animal can see.

Magnetic field the area around a magnetic object where magnetic forces can be felt. Earth has a magnetic field because it contains magnetic metals in its core.

Mandibles jaws.

Mates comes together to breed and create young.

Navigate to find one's way.

Nectar a sugary juice found in the center of a flower's petals.

Ommatidia the units that make up a compound eye.

Pheromones chemicals that are released to send signals to other animals.

Pollen a fine powder that flowers make.

Pollinate when pollen from one flower moves to another flower of the same kind, to make seeds and develop fruit.

Predators animals that hunt other animals to eat.

Simple eyes eyes with only one lens.

Species a type of animal or plant.

Thorax the chest or part of an animal's body between its head and its abdomen.

Ultraviolet (UV) light a form of light energy that humans cannot see.

Vibrations movements up and down and to and fro.

Worker bees the female bees that do all the work in a colony.

Index